# Down My Fairy Stairs

A Door County Poets Collective Book

# Down My Fairy Stairs

Poetry by

Francha Barnard

Edited and Illustrated
by
Elizabeth Ann Barnard

Copyright © 2025 by Elizabeth Ann Barnard

All rights reserved. No part of this publication may be reproduced, distributed or transmitted in any form or by any means, without prior written permission. Without in any way limiting the author's exclusive rights under copyright, any use of this publication to train generative artificial intelligence (AI) technologies to generate text is expressly forbidden.

Cover and interior artwork © 2025 Elizabeth Ann Barnard
Photos © 2025 Neil D. Petta

Four Windows Press

**Four Windows Press**
**231 N. Hudson Ave.**
**Sturgeon Bay, WI 54235**

Publisher's Note: This is a work of poetry. Names, character, places, and incidents are a product of the author's imagination. Locales and public names are sometimes used for poetic purposes. Any resemblance to actual people, living or dead, or to businesses, companies, events, institutions or locates, is completely coincidental.

**Estella Lauter** of the **Door County Poets Collective** helped copy edit this book and regularized punctuation on the basis of long conversations about punctuation in poetry in Word Women meetings and as she and Francha Barnard edited the 2017 Poets Calendar.

Photo credits: Neil D. Petta

**Down My Fairy Stairs** – 1st ed.

ISBN: 979-8-9905946-6-1

# Dedication

To Francha's vast community:

her friends in Door County
and Sheboygan County

her neighbors in Baileys Harbor

all the elementary school children who
benefited from the libraries Francha curated
to foster the love of reading and writing

citizens and tourists of Door County
peninsula,
and tourists, where Francha lived
for seventeen years as a full-time resident,
citizen and literary-activist, and
conservationist as reflected in her generous
support of
The Door County Land Trust
and The Ridges Sanctuary.

# Acknowledgments

Much gratitude to the editors of the following publications in which Francha Barnard's poems previously appeared:

"A Beep and A Wave," 2019 *Wisconsin Poets' Calendar.*
"All I Need," 2016 *Wisconsin Poets' Calendar.*
"Entry," 2018 *Wisconsin Poets' Calendar.*
"Fall Back," 2011 *Wisconsin Poets' Calendar.*
"For Now," Wisconsin Fellowship of Poets, 2018, *Museletter.*
"Good Luck," 2012 *Wisconsin Poets' Calendar.*
"Honor System Shopping," *Halfway to the North Pole.* (Four
    Windows Press).
"Ice Water," 2017 *Wisconsin Poets' Calendar.*
"Living Alone in a Pandemic: Directives," 2021 *Sheltering with
    Poems.* (Wisconsin Fellowship of Poets & Bent Paddle
    Press).
"Necklace," 2013 *Wisconsin Poets' Calendar.*
"Notes to a Novice Observer," 2015 *Wisconsin Poets' Calendar.*
"Ritual," Wisconsin Fellowship of Poets, Fall 2013 *Museletter.*
"Sinking," *The Peninsula Pulse.* Spring 2014, *N.E.W. Voices* Vol 1
    No 4. (Caravaggio Press).
"Tamaracks," *The Peninsula Pulse*, Vol. 17, Issue 20, 2011,
    *Wisconsin Poets' Calendar* 2011.
"The Last Pesto," *N.E.W. Voices* Vol 1 No 2, (Caravaggio Press).
"The Pagami Creek Fire," *The Peninsula Pulse.* Vol 18, Issue 14,
    2012.
"Tomato Ode," 2014 *Wisconsin Poets' Calendar.*
"Warm Day in Early Spring," 2010 *Wisconsin Poet' Calendar.*
"Weavers," *The Peninsula Pulse*, Vol.16, Issue 20, Literary Issue.
    2010, *Soundings*, 2015. (Caravaggio Press).

# Forward

By Elizabeth Ann Barnard

In the beginning, the end was on my mind. One day, before my sister Francha's death in July 2022 but after her cancer diagnosis, I made understated inquiries over the phone as to where she kept an archive of her poems. In her stern librarian voice, and I suppose forbidding expression (you might know it), she cut right through my niceties and said,

"Well, if you're ever looking for them, Elizabeth, they're on my iMac in a folder called "Poems - Mine". Well, that day came when then Poet Laureates of Door County Tom and Ethel Davis, founders of Four Windows Press, in Sturgeon Bay, WI, contacted me expressing interest in publishing a book of Francha's poems. Enormous gratitude to Thomas for giving me this incredible and unforeseen opportunity to give life and legacy to the story of Francha Barnard. It is my great luck and privilege to join the Davises as a flame keeper of Francha's poems. With patience, most of the time, and loving care, I shaped Francha's folder, "Poems – mine," into book form, allowing her voice to be heard once more, and her creative spirit remembered. Francha's unique story unfolds, poem by poem, between the covers of this beautiful book.

When Francha retired to Baileys Harbor in 2005, her shoreline property on Lake Michigan contained a beach and stairs leading down to her happy place. She docked her kayak in the sand and frequently paddled out into the harbor launching her body and mind into freedom to create her poetry. Within 10 years, the shoreline erosion caused her beach to recede and eventually vanish, along with her "fairy stairs". Her poem called "Down My Fairy Stairs" became the title of this book, and an imaginary portal for us to step through and spend an hour or two with Francha.

To create an exhaustive list of Francha's contributions made to the writing community is an impossible task because she touched all four corners of Door County and beyond. Initially, Francha augmented her creative writing efforts by attending a variety of poetry workshops. At the local workshops, Francha caught the attention of the *Word Women* who invited her to join their poetry writing group. She co-edited the *Wisconsin Fellowship of Poets' Calendar* with friend and poet, Estella Lauter, in 2017. She contributed to and worked on two poetry anthologies: *Soundings* and *Halfway to the North Pole* as a member of the Door County Poets Collective.

During a walk from her home to the Baileys Harbor Library, Francha one day got the idea of displaying a local poem each month outside the library door. At the Meadows Art Gallery each Spring, she mounted and often participated in a Poetry and Art exhibit. She volunteered to change the exhibits on the Poetry Trails in Newport State Park each quarter. In addition, the annual program pairing music with poetry called *Words on Fire* benefited from her wholehearted support.

She left her indelible mark on the lives of poets in a program she offered: *Art Speaks*, an ekphrastic writing opportunity that links poetry with works of art at galleries in the area, sponsored by Write On, Door County. Her friend and poet, Ethel Mortenson Davis, Poet Laureate of Door County who still attends "Francha's" ekphrastic writing sessions, honors Francha's memory in her poem: "You Would Be Happy, Francha" in her book *The Woman and The Whale, Encounters with other kingdoms*. Ethel writes: "You would be happy for those gathering today/to relish the essence of you that lingers still." To be honest, reading Ethel's poem and absorbing the sentiment broke me right in two. It makes me feel like Francha is somewhere nearby.

As an early reader, librarian, and educator, Francha became a great reader, taking the necessary first steps to becoming a successful poet. Francha naturally shared her interest in books with friends and fellow educators. She launched the *Baileys Harbor Book Club* in Southern Door County in 2006, and the club still meets monthly. The six to eight members admit that without their stern librarian at the helm, the rules have relaxed a bit. Yes, the book is still the most important thing about the meeting, and you must read the entire book. If you can't attend, you still read the book and submit a written review. BUT instead of limiting the food items to only one, so as to not divert conversation from the book review, the host now may serve two or three items. Despite this rule being bent, I think Francha would be happy that her efforts to marshal readers into a literary community are still thriving

*Down My Fairy Stairs* is a collection of Francha's best poems. I've divided them into six chapters grouped together by Francha's interests in politics, nature, conservation, her personal reflections, and her beloved Door County. The thread that weaves through each chapter and every poem is Francha's sense of community. Francha touched many lives – as a best friend, literary activist, vital City Council Member, helpful neighbor, bird and critter watcher, and energetic organizer. Usually, her poems speak in the first person, revealing an author of great humanity and a voice for the stories of people and creatures who are often brushed aside. And other times, the librarian who read thousands of children's books, gives us a short little ditty about "The Turtle and the Tanker," "The Midge's Lament" or "The Feet Decide." Smile as you remember this Francha who created space for laughter in our lives.

In the end, we are lucky to have a volume of Francha's poetry that allows us to hear her resounding voice telling her unique story. She might say, as she did in her poem, "At the Baileys Harbor Library": "And it's all yours! How luscious is that?!"

Friends of Francha and new readers alike, take a moment to distract yourself from the troubles of life and enter Francha's kingdom of imagination at the bottom of her Fairy Stairs.

With love,

Elizabeth
May 21, 2025

# Editor's Acknowledgements

Our parents, Francis (Frank) and Frances Barnard, who unconditionally loved us and generously shared their talents with their five children, our Father who was a journalist and world news editor for the Sheboygan Press with his love of literature, especially The Bard himself, William Shakespeare, and our Mother who engaged in community activities that made a difference in their local Sheboygan community.

Nancy Rafal, how lucky I am you came to North Carlina to jumpstart the book process. Your experienced poetic eye, and ear, made the initial steps seem like a huge leap forward and have sustained me through this process.

Pam Goode, thank you for including me as a reading only member in Francha's *Baileys Harbor Book Club*. It's meant the world to me to still have this connection to Francha; she often discussed the books you read with me. And thank you for supplying the history of the *Baileys Harbor Book Club* for *Down My Fairy Stairs*.

My son Neil, a big mom hug and huge thank you for being the chronicler of Francha's life through your collection of photos taken during frequent visits to Door County.

Steve Church, my partner and handsome Southern gentleman, who is my rock. Thank you for the hours you spent with me combing through every line of Francha's 300+ poems, not just one time but many. Some of my favorite memories while editing this book will be sitting next to you on the loveseat recliner sharing the same footrest, with the laptop between us, creating the manuscript.

Tom and Ethel Davis, thank you again for making this book a reality for the reading pleasure of Francha's friends, family and future readers. I am in your debt.

My copy editor, Estella Lauter, who worked long hours and dealt with grammar and language challenges to turn these 125 of Francha's poems into their best possible presentation.

Especially, Estella Lauter and The Door County Collective board members whose wholehearted support and enthusiasm buoyed the publication of this beautiful retrospective of Door County's literary advocate, Francha Barnard, in "Down My Fairy Stairs". Many, many thanks.

"Trees are poems that the earth writes upon the sky."

Kahlil Gibran

# Contents

Forward .................................................................................. 9
Editor's Acknowledgements ................................................ 13

## The Rhythm of Waves, Perspectives ................ 23

Down My Fairy Stairs ........................................................ 25
At the Baileys Harbor Library ............................................ 27
The New UU Mic ............................................................... 28
Solstice ............................................................................... 29
Watch the Hands ................................................................ 30
October Morning Imperative ............................................. 31
The Turtle and the Tanker ................................................. 32
Social Isolation ................................................................... 33
Start with Silence ............................................................... 34
Contentment ....................................................................... 35
Living Alone in a Pandemic: Directives ........................... 36
Pin, Baste, Sew ................................................................... 37
Walking ............................................................................... 38
Zen Dressing ....................................................................... 39
Yeast .................................................................................... 40
Lessons: Autumn ................................................................ 41
Notes to a Novice Observer ............................................... 42

## Tomato Ode, A Woman for All Seasons ..........45

Tomato Ode ........................................................................ 47
From Leaden Skies ............................................................ 48
Autumn Pears .................................................................... 49
All I Need .......................................................................... 50
The Last Pesto ................................................................... 51
Clean-up ............................................................................ 52
The Feet Decide ................................................................ 53
Standing in Summer ......................................................... 54
Then Came the Beauty ..................................................... 56
Fizzies ................................................................................ 57
Fall Back ............................................................................ 58
Warm Day in Early Spring ................................................ 59
Winter Comes to Wisconsin ............................................. 60
Noxzema Dreams .............................................................. 61
August Evening Inquiries ................................................. 62
Sound of Sunrise ............................................................... 63
Metamorphosis ................................................................. 64
In Anticipation of Tonight's Snowstorm ......................... 65
Nostalgia ........................................................................... 66
If I Could Choose .............................................................. 67
Cinnamon Season ............................................................. 68
Wind Before the Storm ..................................................... 69
Sweet Light ....................................................................... 70

## War and Peace, Calls to Arms...........................73

Peace and War.................................................................. 75
The Pagami Creek Fire .................................................. 76
School Guns-Wisconsin ................................................. 77
Sarajevo Sorrow .............................................................. 78
Runes of November........................................................ 79
Depth................................................................................ 80
Needed: Cauterization ................................................... 82
Skating on the River of a Million ................................. 83
Hailstorm ........................................................................ 84
Arms Race........................................................................ 85
Playground...................................................................... 86
The Vote .......................................................................... 87
Privacy Priorities ............................................................ 88

## The Midge's Lament, Outdoors Francha......... 91

The Midge's Lament....................................................... 93
Fox Love .......................................................................... 94
August: Rain Needed .................................................... 95
Do You Believe in Omens? ........................................... 96
Leave-taking of the Little Warriors.............................. 97
Water's Work................................................................... 98
Enough............................................................................. 99
Foghorn............................................................................ 100
Garden in a Garden........................................................ 101

Moontangle ................................................................. 102
Sounds of Celebration ............................................... 103
Transcendence ........................................................... 104
Time Warp .................................................................. 105
Beach Babies ............................................................... 106
Junco, an Introvert's Introduction ............................ 108
Nevertheless ............................................................... 109
Affirmation ................................................................. 110
Shape-Shifters/Shade-Changers ............................... 111
The Leave-taking of Filamentous Algae ................. 112
Striped Squirrel Collects a Heart ............................. 113
Great Blue Heron ...................................................... 114
Lookout ....................................................................... 115

# Necklace, A Diary ............................................ 117

Necklace ...................................................................... 119
Love's Last Urgency is Earth .................................... 120
Sitting .......................................................................... 121
As You Go ................................................................... 122
Numbers Woman ...................................................... 123
Unwanted Gifts .......................................................... 124
Veil ............................................................................... 125
Paper Pulp .................................................................. 126
Gravity ........................................................................ 127
Celebration Dinner ................................................... 128
My Dear Women of the Word, ................................ 130

Childhood Saturdays .................................................................. 131
Appetizer ..................................................................................... 132
To the Barre ................................................................................ 133
Siren Call .................................................................................... 134
Sinking ........................................................................................ 136
Adopted ....................................................................................... 137
First Library ................................................................................ 138
Expiration Date: A Brief Encounter ......................................... 140
Old Blue Patchwork ................................................................... 141
Section B ..................................................................................... 142
Old Cat ........................................................................................ 144
The Seatmate .............................................................................. 145
This Year's Letter ........................................................................ 147

## Will's Summer People, Door County ............. 149

Will's Summer People ................................................................ 151
A Beep and a Wave .................................................................... 152
Overlooked ................................................................................. 153
Weavers ....................................................................................... 154
May Ritual .................................................................................. 155
At Hidden Brook ........................................................................ 156
Tamaracks ................................................................................... 158
Walking Home from Shakespeare ............................................ 159
Fog-marked Morning ................................................................ 160
Dancing Cows ............................................................................ 161
A Sensual Sunset ........................................................................ 162

Honor System Shopping ............................................................. 163
The Neighbor's Cows ................................................................. 164
Zukes and Cukes........................................................................ 165
Certainty..................................................................................... 166
Tuesday, 4:32 a.m. ..................................................................... 167
Pencil in Hand............................................................................ 168
Just Before the Hunt ................................................................. 169
Talisman ..................................................................................... 170
Survivor...................................................................................... 171
I Do Begrudge Losing ............................................................... 173
Dappled Days............................................................................. 173


About the Author ...................................................................... 175
About the Illustrator ................................................................. 176

# The Rhythm of Waves
Perspectives

Francha Barnard

## Down My Fairy Stairs

*remembering my stairs down to Lake Michigan*

Eighteen steps down
another life unfolded;
at the base of narrow wooden stairs
half the world before me,
half the world behind,
backed by twenty feet of dolomite limestone
rife with fossils from the Silurian Sea
that filled this Lake Michigan basin eons ago.

Ahead, the edge of the bay
rimmed my tiny town;
sky and water offered a palette
of blues, grays and greens
depending on the season,
depending on the weather,
depending on the day,
depending on the time.

Life around me there could be
amused by buffleheads in early spring
mergansers all summer long,
goldeneyes in autumn.
It was replete with gulls and terns,
accented with pelicans
and swans sometimes,
and occasionally, even an eagle.,

Down the stairs,
absent from the human world,
away from its incessant clamor

## Down My Fairy Stairs

no one knew that I was there
mornings with coffee,
evenings with, perhaps, a glass of wine
and always slow, slow thoughts
enfolded in the rhythm of waves.

Francha Barnard

# At the Baileys Harbor Library

Your anticipation rises
as you enter the tiny two rooms
of your town's library halfway up the peninsula.

Today you browse, choose,
sit to read a bit
…and the walls fall away, the ceiling recedes.

You're hiking the Highlands in Scotland,
building the Panama Canal,
rolling on a whaler in the Atlantic,
sneaking through the garden's secret gate,
picking blueberries for Sal.

This place can manipulate magic,
can carry you away on a deep cozy chair
at the price of zero.

This place can bring tears, laughter, fear
between the covers in your hands.

This place tickles your funny bone,
twists your temper, pulls at your heart.

And it's all yours!  How luscious is that?!

# The New UU Mic

### 1

When, months ago, the UU installed
a new mic for the congregation,
they gave the poets
who frequent this dais
a gift of great proportion.

### 2

We who live by words,
tiptoe ideas onto the page,
require one final task for closure;
live by the premise *your poem
isn't done until its shared.*

### 3

Can a machine make one a better poet?
This new mic pulls me to the podium
I move; it follows my voice,
wings it to eager ears in the audience
creates a world with
               no
                     lost
                             words.

Francha Barnard

## Solstice

Even on this shortest day
feather moss – Brachythecium
that roofs the rocks
on trails in the forest —
seems to glow
chartreuse from within.

It may be the fairies
hidden in the dolomite
who've gathered to dance
around their lighted fires
making heat that's
warming the mosses.

Though they mean
to send no message,
perhaps we should heed
the fairies' choice:
gather, light fires,
dance.

# Watch the Hands

*Birchwood Art, Scandia Village*

They begin each week, as they have for years,
(save the precious time that Covid stole)
paint near paper,
fingers holding brush handles,
sometimes just above the ferrule.
They load paint on brush tips
and land, like birds, on the paper,
some diving, some approaching *very* slowly,
some fluttering down.

Wide swaths and tiny dabs, designer lines and scrubs,
the artists of Birchwood bring white to life
and even for those whose speech has been stolen,
they're telling stories.
Watch the hands.

Francha Barnard

# October Morning Imperative

wake early
stand at the screen

wait

you will
be rewarded

look
just now
at the trees
at the point of land's end
across the bay


each trunk, branch
silhouetted
against the saffron backdrop
of the sun's
rising

at this moment
now

# The Turtle and the Tanker

When you spot,
on a single afternoon,
a box turtle on the trail
and a tanker in big water,
the lesson is indisputable;
there's beauty in going slow.

Francha Barnard

# Social Isolation

Time becomes malleable
when you're confined to your home–
hard enough when you're ill,
harder still when you're healthy.

If, these days, there rests in you
a deep well of fear or melancholy,
leave the shore and go into the woods
where bare deciduous fingers scratch the sky.

And in your silence,
your silence,
hear overt exuberant birdsong,
hear singing purely for this day,
this day.

Let it buoy you and guide you home.

## Start with Silence

There is a house
on a bluff at a lake
where two cats lived, lounged,
then languished as old age overcame them,
until the day came there was only one cat,
until the day came there were none.

If silence has weight,
the air in this house bent under it then.
Ears could hear—silence.
Bodies swam through it
until it bore down so hard,
breathing itself became a heavy task.

Only one way to alleviate it,
only one way to lift this pall—
a tiny new kitten arrived
bringing her gift of weightlessness
to stir the air again.

Francha Barnard

## Contentment

This mild December morning,
stand very still and listen
on this Lake Michigan bluff.

Listen long enough to hear
ducks rafting in calm water below
purring to each other.

# Living Alone in a Pandemic: Directives

*Door County, WI*

Do not allow loneliness to sit in your lap.
Eschew empty hours (though sitting still is not necessarily
    empty).
Look to all that is good in your life.

It's July.
    Waves lap the shore, a rhythm for your day.
    The moon's been particularly gracious lately.
    You live in a version of nirvana.
    Your neighbors are a knock away,
    far-flung family and friends, the distance of a phone
    call.

Use time
    to sit in your glider
    watch hummingbirds drink
    read—really read
    make art, music, poetry
    walk beside nature
        in the height of its prime
    eat meals on the porch
    sleep with all the windows open
    awaken daily to wren song and gull cry.

Do not think about fall and winter.
They'll arrive when they arrive.

Francha Barnard

# Pin, Baste, Sew

As children learning to create clothing
we early memorized the mantra, "pin, baste, sew".
We mastered the loose running stitch
as we fitted sleeves, seams, pleats, darts.
We knew a more perfect product would emerge
because of that careful threaded middle step.

I'm thinking now of Neem basting[1] shows together
for years in the park, on the road,
my mother's expertise in applying the threads
that made perfect fits, invisible to us,
each lucky audience who saw
only the finished project,
the ensuing magic.

---

[1] Neem basting is a temporary basting method used to hold fabric layers together before final stitching.

# Walking

Walking doesn't have
to take
you somewhere.

Walking
can just
take you.

Francha Barnard

# Zen Dressing

To begin a weaving
bend over the loom
choose one measured thread
that you've placed on the beam.
Reach around; pull it through
the reed's first tiny slit. Repeat
at the next.
Repeat.
Repeat
maybe two hundred times
'til you've used every thread.

You've now half completed
preparing to weave.
Move to the loom's back.
Bend over again.
Begin to pull threads
through the tiny-holed heddles.
Repeat.
Repeat
until all threads are strung.

You've now,
if you've chosen,
made dressing the loom
your own meditation.

# Yeast

My mother's days
were defined by what she baked.

Danish, crescent rolls, clovers,
sticky buns, all manner of breads.
Yeast was her milieu.
Back in her kitchen corner,
her floured hands would
mix, roll, pat and brush
while I stood at her side
absorbing by osmosis
the feel of the dough
when it had risen,
learning her lesson,
Handle lightly – only
as much as you need to.

Now my mother lives on in my hands.

Francha Barnard

# Lessons: Autumn

Look how the leaf bears no grudge for being released by the
 tree,
and the tree no grudge for being deprived of its finery;

how the monarch bears no grudge for its thousand-mile
 journey,
the migrating cranes, for relinquishing their summer homes;

how the red squirrel doesn't begrudge her hours spent storing
 winter nuts,
nor the chickadee hers used to stash seeds;

how the bullfrog surrenders summer's sun-warmed water,
just burrows deeper to let winter's torpor take over.

So, why do I begrudge afternoon's early daylight loss?

## Notes to a Novice Observer

      There
at the top of the dying birch
the one down the road
hanging over the bluff
with only two branches
still reaching for sky

there sits that crow
telling his black story
his film noir   danse macabre
in raspy dire words
of lifelong complaint;
a one-crow cacophony

do you see him there?
if not see him, at least hear?

# Tomato Ode
# A Woman for All Seasons

Francha Barnard

# Tomato Ode

To you who give so freely
of seed and pulp and juice;
to you who let your skin be pricked
and sliced and cubed and peeled;
to you who stew, puree and roast;
to you of green and orange and puce;
to you who tart my tongue,
who lush my mouth,
who drip my chin,

I nod my humble thanks.

# From Leaden Skies

lozenges of snow drop from leaden skies,
bigger flakes than ever seen.

the earth grows white–
then whiter than before

on this day that should have
brought rain.

Francha Barnard

# Autumn Pears

They line the windowsill to ripen
wait for sun and time to soften them
their shapes and sizes various
their interiors formed from similar seed

Although they grew on the same tree
came to this moment in like season
each is singular in its essence
each alone though yet aligned

The smallest one saw decline first
the middle rolled in its own direction
the third centered late and then stood firm
these three daughters of our mother

# All I Need

in this Wisconsin winter that seems determined
to walk out at its own slow pace,
is a single augury, an unmistakable emissary:
sunset after six,
a cardinal's morning mate-searching call,
snowdrop blossoms in a sun-hollowed bowl,
or, best, a foolish winter-hearty robin –
orange and brown at the edge of this white world.

Francha Barnard

# The Last Pesto

Though July is generous
yielding tender young leaves
for the oil and pine nuts,

and August's abundance
surrenders its growth,
wanting only to blossom,

it's hard-earned September
whose harvest I love best.
Basil, my darling persnickety plants,

whose leaves, insect eaten,
will blacken at first frost,
now begs to be much trimmed

and blended with garlic,
then sun-dried tomatoes
to sweeten the greens;

this last pungent batch
offers freezer-bag bounty
through winter's vast white.

## Clean-up

There is that interlude
in March
when snow is gone
but cold remains....
when the urge
to work in the yard
outvotes common sense

Francha Barnard

# The Feet Decide

Today will be a heavy-sock day
black alpaca, I think, should do it
for snow-blowing that awaits,
the long drive buried in three new inches.

I'll follow that task with cocoa by the fire,
toes pointed toward the warming flame,
cold, even in alpaca after an hour outside.

And now, to muse, to plan ahead,
Tonight's a concert, dress-up fancy,
thin-ribbed cotton wrapping my feet
in, I know it already, insufficient heat.

No, that won't be, I feel too good
with toes ensconced in quilted warmth.
The feet decide; I'm staying home.

# Standing in Summer

*Poem written after Carl Vanderheyden's sculpture "First Steps"*

Early in summer in a tiny field
the foal sits beside a garden
where his mother birthed him this morning,
soft face looking with wonder at his back legs
as if they weren't attached to him,
as if his body ended at his haunches.

How can he know that it's time to try
to lift himself somehow,
to join this wondrous world he's entered
to explore its corners and hedgerows?

And he's not alone—
other long legs in the forest, newborn,
are also lifting their spotted backs
and wobbling behind their mothers
through brush and trees;
baby foxes are gamboling
just outside their cave homes,
tousling with siblings on stubby legs,
standing falling, rolling,
as, back in the field
the foal leans forward, kneels,
spreads rear legs wide and
pushes himself back toward them
so his front feet can gain purchase
in the unfamiliar dirt.

Now he takes tentative steps
on skinny, shaking limbs;

never again will this be so hard,
so foreign,
this walk toward freedom.

# Then Came the Beauty

After a day of rising temps
and rain on roads transformed to ice,
evening fell to snow – big flakes and wet
and long night obscured it all.

Then came the beauty of Tuesday morning:

a child's art project, all glue and cotton,
fluff on every trunk and limb,
pink sky at sunrise – lone crow striping the view,
diamond dust drifting on a tiny breeze,

white carpet lightly pocked as
limbs above let go their temporary tenants:
a world gone clean     and soft
          and kind.

Francha Barnard

# Fizzies

If I squint my eyes
I can travel through time
back to my childhood, 1950's.

Into the view master
I slip a disk
marked "Summer 1952"
I click to a cellophane
of five little tykes
moving from the shallows
water streaming from them
as they dash across hot sand
for the shelter
of the beach house.

Screen door slams
as they climb on benches
that surround the table.

Now cast in a sand coating,
short legs dangle down
swing in silent rhythms
anticipating the moment.
They each take a glass
of anodized shine
drop in a fizzy and
peer over the top edge
watch water turn to pop,
well, at least its close relative.

Then they down the first gulp
as bubbles fill their noses,
such treats, such little miracles.

# Fall Back

It is never OK
To take away my afternoon
And tack it onto morning:
To take away halcyon
And add, instead, efficient.

I know, I know…
The light fits better to the day.
But, still,
You've shrouded me in mourning;
You've caused a little death.

Francha Barnard

# Warm Day in Early Spring

Go ahead, lovely lady,
swish your skirts.
Show us a little ankle.

Tease us with
some decolletage.
Let a bit of sleeve
fall from your shoulder.

Lull us, charming coquette,
with your simpering murmurs;
your sidelong glances.

We'll take your promises,
your hide-and-seek game,
your momentary gift.

But we won't be fooled
by your coltish ways.
Soon you'll not just
sashay past.

One day you'll ring the bell
and waltz right in
for tea and a long chat.

# Winter Comes to Wisconsin

*Poem written after Jeff Boutin's oil painting
"Calm Waters"*

What happened to summer—
to lush leaves and verdant grass,
to insistent sun reflecting
on golden sand and azure water,
to languorous days; the luxury
of lying on a beach towel,
of splashing in wavelets?

All replaced by this—
sere yellows, tans, grays
along the shore we now walk,
bundled in jackets and boots,
stocking caps pulled down tight,
our fingers muffled in mittens
as we clap our hands warm.

Even the rocks, just wading at water's edge,
wear a top sheen of new snow,
and tutus of thin ice pirouette
in slow circles on solemn water;
a reminder that the rolling calendar
seasons our days,
invites the ever-new to our senses.

## Noxzema Dreams

Beach babies that we were,
the scent of summer,
especially at evening in our house was of Noxzema.

The blue jar held in our mother's hand,
its white cream on the fingers of the other was liberally lathered
on the backs and shoulders
of my redheaded siblings
whose skin by that time
had turned burning scarlet,
whose discomfort at being touched
even gently
was audible throughout the house.

Later, they'd fitfully slumber
on clouds of its vapor,
that medicinal mint
shimmering from sheets and pillowcases to wake the next day,

beach time on their minds.

## August Evening Inquiries

If I breathed in tonight's summer-ending breeze,
would its warmth wrap me through the winter ahead?

If I caught in a jar these lolling waves,
would they still roll to my listening ear?

If I closed my eyes to the Milky Way,
would starlight seep beneath my eyelids?

If I cut open tonight's just-rising orange moon,
would it drip sweet juice onto my tongue?

If tonight were all I had of life, would it be enough?

Francha Barnard

# Sound of Sunrise

On this first fall day
she rises before dawn
to face east on the porch
coffee in hand
to be part of the sun's welcome
across the bay,
a leavening of one.

The dawn's second gift:
the thrum/whirr of crane's wings
just over her head
a simple ancient "cwak"
from the leader of five.

# Metamorphosis

The sun has finally
turned her face upon us.

Chestnut leaf-chicks
burst their eggshell buds.

Birches' skinny, red-polished fingers
massage the lapis sky.

Contorted filberts' limey catkins
curtsy in the breeze.

New saffron willow tendrils
sway to silent music

as the season of fullness unfolds.
We have waited long and long.

Francha Barnard

# In Anticipation of Tonight's Snowstorm

It is enough

to awaken to the sight of five cranes
flying in a line—north

to walk the lake bluff road
in midafternoon in a strong wind,
gulls wheeling above, conversing as they fly,
ice sheets crinkling in the water below
as they climb atop one another

to note the sun's valiant effort
to outshine thickening clouds

to be given these hours

of anticipation, of observation,
of surrender to what will surely come.

# Nostalgia

not so grand as grief
these wisps of summer past
early breakfasts on the porch
sunlight nibbling on bare shoulders,
tomatoes eaten off the plant
while standing at the raised bed's edge,
bare feet dangling in warm lake water
latest book choice in my hands,
rosy sunset at nearly nine
leading languid day to bed

Francha Barnard

# If I Could Choose

Let me die in early October.
Let me lie back in this lush bed
of sun-struck reds and ochres.

Let the wafting breeze
release russets and rusts
from their tenuous hold.

Let the ducks rafting nearby
in the cooling lake water
softly chat while I listen.

In this golden light,
let the last thing my eyes see
be these bountiful trees.

# Cinnamon Season

It's almost the season of cinnamon. I can sense it in the air:

needing to don socks with shoes; not the thin ones either,
sweaters in the early morning and again at evening's blush,
chatty shaking of getting-ready-to-drop leaves,
petal-less flowerheads nodding in browned gardens

and in the orchards: russet, rouge, ruby and red-gold.

Now rise delicious daydreams of crisps and rustic apple pies,
of fruit-stuffed pork tenderloins, ragouts and rice pudding,
comfort foods as our part of the earth tilts from the sun
and we arm ourselves with cinnamon for the season ahead.

Francha Barnard

# Wind Before the Storm

All night she circles
        Snapping,
        Snarling,
Sinister, intemperate.

She lunges forward
        Grabbing,
        Clawing,
Scratching at our eyelid's edge.

Her fury gathers
        Raging,
        Roaring,
Omnipresent in the dark.

# Sweet Light

What meager sun there was today
shone early
and then for five minutes only
before it collapsed
under a sheet of gray

And yet,

and yet – in those few moments
it spewed pinks and oranges and golds
onto the ice floes in the bay
fondant enough to sweeten
the hours of rain that ensued

# War and Peace
# Calls to Arms

Francha Barnard

## Peace and War

Here the sky is a riot
of pinks and lavenders,
oranges and fuchsias
as we wait for the sun
to peek above a watery horizon,
send its welcoming path of light
across gently undulating waves.

There the sky is black with smoke
—a nuclear plant, a hospital, a kindergarten
hit by rocket bombs
intentionally aimed for utter destruction
while millions flee their homes to escape
unjustified attack
by one malevolent man.

If only my tears could take you home
they'd float you back today
to a house that still stands,
to a village of friends
to a country at peace.

# The Pagami Creek Fire

I'm thinking of the fish today,
of deer and voles
and porcupines.

Their spirits rode on smoke that we,
a state away,
inhaled all night.

Don't believe the news reports
that say there were
no casualties.

Francha Barnard

# School Guns—Wisconsin

Do we need in school another class
this one the height of hypocrisy,
touted, though, for "increased safety"?
Already 23 have signed
onto the bill now in the Assembly.

The offer: in school, let's teach gun use;
handguns to rifles in 2017-18.
Let's use our tax dollars
not for roads, not for healthcare, not for teachers.
Let's use them for gun safety.

Some of us already choose
early evenings dining out
before "social" drinking gets heavy,
aware that there are handguns
in pockets and purses around us.

To propose that teens should learn *guns*
as part of their normal school day
must be a cruel trick of absurdist comedy,
especially when the bill's writer remarks,
"(shooting) is fun, just like attending a baseball game".

Only it's not.

## Sarajevo Sorrow

How could they ravage
Saint Josip's this way?
Destroying the altar,
revealing its monstrance,
crushing the statues –
bitter salt of this war.

And here on its side
rests this broken chalice –
wine-holder, blood-holder,
now cruelly boot-stomped
beside primrose blossoms –
forgiving first flowers of spring.

Even the soft lime green grass
of this city,
my Sarajevo,
my torn heart's love,
will never grow over
this rash pagan act.

Francha Barnard

# Runes of November

*"these are signs [everyone else is telling stories]"*
*Diane Di Prima "Alchemical Signs"*

the late fall sun warming my face
the ghostly gurgle of water-tumbled rocks
       in wind-bewitched waves
the back of a red fox baby, now all grown,
       crossing the yard under my window
a lilypad-munching muskrat
       swimming in Solitude Swale
three sandhill cranes
       their long bodies dipping low
       over my car on County S
a looseness the day after the election
       bones and sinew relaxing
       after four knotted years
a passing smile beneath a Covid mask

I share these signs with you
       my fellow traveler in turbulent times

# Depth

Some years ago a president
not particularly known for his depth
declared that no child would be left behind
and so began a war on education
giving rise, as some would call them,
to the *chanting schools*.

In came dates and famous names,
arcs and angles,
the periodic table,
countries and capitals:
all memorized and regurgitated,
sometimes in choral unison.

Out went
nuance,
creativity,
imagination,
discussion, debate, opinion:
REAL education.

Some months ago a governor
not particularly known for his depth
declared Wisconsin "open for business"
and so began a war in my state.

In came cuts for all of us
except the rich and powerful;
less money for health care and
women and kids;
as if our worth were less
than the wealthy's.

Francha Barnard

Out went
bargaining together,
voting without a photo ID,
Family Care dollars and
publicly-owned utilities:
life as we'd known it in our state.

This is a poem without an end,
for we in Wisconsin don't yet understand
where these choices will take us
and who'll be broken in their wake.

# Needed: Cauterization

For all her life
the tunnel of trees
on the road through
the Jacksonport Swamp
signaled *nearly there*
nearly to grandpa's, then
nearly to her cottage,
later, to her own home.

This morning
the DC Highway crew
and their hired hitmen
amputated the tunnel,
buzz sawed roadside trees
down to 10-inch stumps,
inadvertently
nicked her heart.

Francha Barnard

# Skating on the River of a Million

Did you eat your Wheaties this morning, Scott Walker,
your   HUMPF    breakfast of champions?

Did you drink your fortified orange juice to stiffen your spine;
down your caffeine-filled coffee to jump-start your tiny heart?

Did you shower, dry and pat on the gunpowder
that's available in pockets all over the state now?

Did you shave off those black, cynical whiskers
and lacquer your hair with a veneer of compassion?

Did you don your armor of lies and open the door
to much colder Wisconsin air today?

Did you set out skating on the river of a million recall names
to work at the Statehouse that's not the people's house
anymore?


Careful, Scott Walker, the ice is cracking;
your armor is dragging you under.

# Hailstorm

We saw it Tuesday
on the morning news;
the Monday hail, handfuls of it—
some baseball-sized,
spit from the sky
at Hillside Orchard and beyond,
had dented cars,
damaged machinery
and sent the owner,
last to leave the orchard,
for eight stitches to his headwound.

The apples, ripe now for picking,
were bruised and torn a bit
by the smaller hail globes,
the bigger ones rolled off the apples—
less harm done.

Hail like this mid-September event
used to be rare
used to be isolated to tiny pockets
used to be the subject of jocular fish tales.

Now, though, as our weather grows
more inclined to anger
more inclined to excess
you can almost see the earth wince,
hear her sharp, shocked *ouch*.

You realize *something's* changing.
You know you had a part in this.
You hope you can undo it.

Francha Barnard

# Arms Race

*arbalest: a medieval crossbow with a steel drawstring*

Early Welsh archers loosed their arrows
the arbalest later sent them farther

and all the while they called for peace

the blunderbuss with smoke and fire
cannonballs at Chancellorsville
chlorine gas in Flanders Fields
Paris, London felled by planes

and still they called for peace

Nagasaki, Hiroshima under
singing wings of atomic bombs
Aleppo, Mosul – new ghostly ruins
as silent drones drop lethal payloads

and still we call for peace

All the years,
all the lives,
all the waste

and still we can't

toe over the line
–paper thin–
from war to peace.

# Playground

This is a literal poem
a lament
and a warning.

At recess this morning
demeaning names were called,
bullies cornered little ones,
wheelchairs were "accidentally" bumped,
fifth grade girls were chased and surrounded,
wildy boys scorning them,
because tacit permission's been given
by the votes last night of their elders.

This is a literal poem
a warning
        and a lament.

Francha Barnard

## The Vote

Locked
left out
made to wait
wait for mail
await a ballot
blamed for missing
one blank line
dismissed for lacking
proper ID

Boxes subtracted
ballots undeposited
lines too long
sun too hot
turned away
couldn't stay
to have our say

What kind of country
will we be
without democracy?

# Privacy Priorities

Why, I wonder, librarian that I am,
is the country apoplectic
since the media found out
that collection in secret
of our phone calls
(where? when?)
can be ordered by judges?

BUT

after 9/11
when the same data gathering
could be forced on librarians
and, mind you, in absolute secret
for check-out records
of suspected patrons—
hardly a public peep was heard.

Why do the words that you read
appear to be not as private
as your chat with a neighbor
or a faraway friend?

# The Midge's Lament
## Outdoors Francha

## The Midge's Lament

because we travel in the aggregate
you think us a nuisance at best
but take a minute     we don't bite
Put your nose up close
I'll sit on this window so you can study
my ephemeral beauty

graceful long black-stockinged legs
each finer than one human hair
bushy antennae on my brothers
hence our nickname "fuzzy bills"
diaphanous wings so slight and light
we ride the tiniest updrafts

try to think of me as
Spring's sacrificial lamb
I'm food for fish and birds
and water bugs     but
if you just keep your mouth closed
I won't be food for you

# Fox Love

My little ones
just leaving the den
have learned to worship
the morning sun

They spread themselves
on rocks and roots
in tiny undulations.
Do they yet know it's life they love?

Francha Barnard

# August:  Rain Needed

What we need
is a good shower,
long and slow,
maybe lasting all morning
or, better yet,
night-long,
no wind.

You know the kind;
one that
      saturates
      irrigates
      satiates
the thirsty ground;
      ameliorates
the dust that
      slithers between our toes
      irritates our eyes
      sleeps with us in our sheets.

Perfect would be
hours and hours
of gentle weeping
from the sky
until the sadness
of this dry earth
evaporates.

# Do You Believe in Omens?

You stand at the glass,
watch dawn open
on the far horizon
– diluted carmines and oranges.

At just above freezing,
the lake water is thick today.

The clock on a nearby wall
ratchets the minutes….
an ordinary early morning,
albeit in subtle tiers of beauty.

And then
                and then

just above the sluggish waves
an eagle       skims          smoothly      by

and this day is christened.

Francha Barnard

# Leave-taking of the Little Warriors

Who would think
when all summer long
they daily appear
seeking red, seeking sweet water,
whirring and beeping,
hovering and attacking,
shivering sun from their iridescent shoulders,
as they chase each other from feeder to tree,
that one silent morning
they'd just not be here?

# Water's Work

*Poem written after Steven Haas Mobile
"Holey Stones"*

They lie there, they fly here
these seven stones with holes,
these imperfect relics
from an ancient world,
now wire-hung to drift in air,
then wave-rolled round
in a time before time.

And in due time
when humans found them,
they found them useful.
They lifted stones to build
their homes, their roads, their towns.

And in due time
they carved statues in mountainsides
in roadside shrines
made altars in rustic churches
and arching cathedrals.

And in due time
they assigned stones power
those they prayed to
and those they turned in a hand—
a mantra—thought or softly spoken—
even now, making stones holy.

Francha Barnard

# Enough

*"Nobody can outguess the future."*
*Haruki Murakami*

This mid-May afternoon
the floor of the forests is full of trillium,
in nearby corrals,
new fillies are feeding from their mothers,
a cultivator, even on this Sunday,
is churning up the soil for planting
while the lake sends rippled wavelets to shore.

It is enough.
It is enough.

# Foghorn

To a landlubber
Growing up at water's edge,
The foghorn's bass note
Sounds not a warning, but a reassurance
That all is well, all continues.

Its presence is enough
To set the tone, the pace.
It repeats for so many months, years,
That it becomes the undercurrent,
The beat of a life.

So, too, with you, dear friends.
Your presence is enough
To set the tone, the pace,
For a landlubber
Hoping to grow old at water's edge.

Francha Barnard

# Garden in a Garden

*Bjorklunden, Lawrence University*

Just feet from the Bard's leafy stage
where his words wrap summer nights
in love and chaos,
lies a small rectangle of symmetry.

Gates on four sides of a low wooden wall
beckon entry to a garden, now fading.
Trimmed boxwood hedge-balls
line paths to a center left open of plantings.

The daisies have finished —
mere pods now on dry poles,
but anemones remain, pirouetting their pinks,
nodding on their three-foot stems.
And lavender still scents the air.

Two statues undertake their daily tasks—
a cherub basketing pomegranates,
a young woman ferrying water in a jug.

Two benches welcome the visitor
to sit, to be lulled to quiet
here in this small corner of order
in a world of growing disorder.

# Moontangle

She rises tonight
from her waterbed
Lake Michigan's waves
gone calm
gone cobalt
gone cold

She's just freed herself
from dark tree tangles
from birch branches trying
to hold her close
to keep her near
to own her light

The birches sense
her disdain for earth
her need for open sky
but still they grasp
at her shifting shape
tonight ripe round

But she wrests herself
from their reaching arms
this won't be the night
the birches hold her
this won't be the night
she'll stay.

Francha Barnard

# Sounds of Celebration

Curled brittle maple and oak leaves
scuttle along the patchwork road.
A high wind coughs and sneezes
through the white pines and cedars,
rubs close trunks and branches,
extorting groans and scritches.

Ice floes crack and crack again,
assemble a new jigsaw puzzle
along the nearby beach's edge.

I breathe star points of crystalline air,
my chin tucked deep inside my collar

# Transcendence

It is a good thing
that I go alone sometimes
into these woods
that crouch close to my home.

And it makes no matter
whether snowshoed or clog-clad,
in this tangle
of tamarack and cedar and white pine,

there comes a moment
as I pause on these paths,
an exquisitely light moment
in the silence that is not silent,

when there is no me;
    there is only
        everything
            else.

Francha Barnard

# Time Warp

*(on the day I returned from Spain)*

tangerine moon drowns
in the western pre-dawn sky
of Barcelona

rises in the evening
from lake Michigan's water
crimson, living still

# Beach Babies

The beaches we five swam
span two hundred miles,
Sheboygan in Wisconsin
to Ford River near Escanaba,
all waters of the same long lake
—Michigan—whimsical
mistress of our hearts.

That lake was steps away
at Hidden Brook in Baileys Harbor—
just out the front door and
down a path past the beach house
at Villa Loch Ree in the UP—
a two-block walk through alleys
and down 88 steps
to a lifeguarded beach
in Sheboygan.

We knew our lake's smiles and her frowns.
We feared her anger with good reason.
She could turn in a minute,
sometimes beguile you,
hide her undertow in silence
or offer up big, fast waves
for dangerous rollicking.

We had a lot of freedom then.
Our parents would send us alone
knowing we were safe and watched.
As kids we were taught to respect our lake,
as teens we often defied that lesson,
swam out beyond safety to fishing net buoys
in games of "Touch the Red".

Francha Barnard

It will always be summer in memory.
We'll always be wearing swimsuits,
the sand and waves of Michigan,
our lodestone.

## Junco, an Introvert's Introduction

I'm the neighborhood shy-child
not usually inserting myself among others,
though chickadees, who match my size,
sometimes share my space.

Not a loud-mouth, I,
nor a flashy dresser either.
In my dun gray and white habit
you might think me one
from an avian order of nuns.

Nor is my routine assertive.
I tend to flit when I fly
and two-foot hop forward and back
when I'm ground-bound where
I prefer to eat seeds fallen from your feeder.

I'm always on the lookout for you.
So look for me in winter    and listen, too,
for my unassuming Arctic Circle one-note
a lament for my summer home way north.

I don't regret my reticence.
It's largely what defines me.

Francha Barnard

# Nevertheless

I never lived on a river, Lorine[2];
no spring floods made my home a boat.
My father never fished for carp,
nor mother suffered deafness.
I never had a Zukie bring me 'round to poets
or chose still to return to poverty and mud.

And yet I know them through you,
know your Black Hawk Island,
know mist, know birdsong, flowers,
know war and pain and silence –
especially the silence of spaces
in the cacophony of words.

---

[2] Lorine Niedecker

# Affirmation

*...that light is an invitation to happiness, when it's done right, is a kind of holiness, palpable and redemptive.*

*Mary Oliver*
*"Poppies"*

After days and days of cold,
days of our piece of earth
crusted over with snow and ice,
the sun stood up from her cloudbank chair
to waltz across our bay's frozen face
and smile—ah, smile upon us.

Yes, say maple limbs, crystal-swathed
yes, say nuthatches and chickadees who flit to the feeder
yes, say juncos dining on terrace-scattered seeds
yes, say we who look on them,
we are blessed by all this light
on our piece of frozen earth.

Francha Barnard

## Shape-Shifters/Shade-Changers

Waves have been my lifelong daily companions;

I've floated on their soothing aqua surfaces
and feared their indigo might.
They've swathed me in the Florida Keys,
nearly crushed me in Trinidad.
They've nibbled my feet at the Jersey shore,
half frozen me in Lake Michigan.
They've offered up oysters in Washington state
swum me with tiny tetras in Mexico.

Foaming azure carnival rides of my childhood,
cobalt rhythms of my aging days,
their motion is my backdrop,
they'll hold me when I die.

# The Leave-taking of Filamentous Algae

*a.k.a. clydophora*

No one would call the scent of clydophora pleasant,
but on the day Lake Michigan's hungry whitecaps
break up shoreline green-topped ice floes
and winter-trapped algae is swallowed back to sea,
on THAT day, for those who live at the shore,
the fading fragrance of clydophora is sweet perfume.

Francha Barnard

# Striped Squirrel Collects a Heart

A new neighbor's moved in,
more handsome than most
and compact as well,
though he holds his own
with the reds and grays.

In his banker-striped suit
white stitches between,
he assays his surroundings
his head peeking out
from the eco-home he's bought
amid lush greens on terraces.

Squinny--his Iowa nickname
and mine now for him
amiably chats as he shops for seeds,
scours the ground around the feeder
picks up what he needs
to put away for the future.

Unlike the famous grasshopper of fable,
Squinny's got a long-term plan.
I hope he winters over here
and we'll become close friends.
For now, I am besotted.

# Great Blue Heron

All arms and legs and neck,
you lift off from the creek
to enter another dimension
though none who study physics
would wager on your success.

Francha Barnard

# Lookout

If it were on the ocean,
this could be the prow
of a giant vacation liner;
observation decks – layer on layer.

Instead it stands unmoving
in the forest's verdant depths,
a maple trunk, tall, straight, old
dressed in layers of shelf fungi;

laddered observation decks still,
but for fairies on guard duty
who use them to detect
*any* who would approach in disbelief.

# Necklace
# A Diary

Francha Barnard

## Necklace

little sapling white pine
barely tall as I am
trunk only round
as my extended thumb

you wear a pearl necklace
even so –
after last night's
windless snow

# Love's Last Urgency is Earth

*after Christian Wiman*

I grow old and weary at times
of living with a body that can disappoint,
leave me dwelling in illusion.

Around me, friends and family are dying,
their bodies returning to dust,
their memory, for me, a weight I carry.

Though its time dwells in the unknown,
I turn now to thoughts of my own final rest,
my own return to this generous earth.

Francha Barnard

# Sitting

He wasn't the kind of dad who played—
not a ball-tosser or active swimmer
not a hugger or hold-close guy.

Rather, I remember him sitting,
reading evenings in the master bedroom,
American histories or sometimes,
Shakespeare delivered aloud.

When we five were very young,
he'd sit evenings on the bottom bunk
to read us poems and bedtime stories
or he'd sing—we learned all the military tunes.

He sat for work, too,
editing AP and UPI stories for our newspaper
rolling in his chair to the teletypes behind him,
then rolling back with more news to edit.

As we grew, he became our editor
We'd troop upstairs from the kitchen homework table
finished, we'd think, paper in hand
for his eyes to catch errors and kindly correct us.

Conversely, he was always a walker,
a couple of miles a day after work,
probably for a peaceful respite
before home's hubbub of children's noise.

And here am I, older now than he then,
walking and reading,
his passions now mine.

## As You Go

It isn't fair is it
to begrudge you this –
this going first,

your tired bones, war-pocked, finally resting,
those bullet-born migraines ended,
your fire for tomorrow extinguished?

Now you can float over
scarlet maples on sunny French hillsides,
waste dappled hours and no one will chide you.

So
what is this tear smudge, this tiny concession,
I wipe from my cheek when no one is looking?

Francha Barnard

# Numbers Woman

Maybe she thought that
if she knew enough of them
she could build a stack
to the shortcut door
in heaven's keel.

Sister Agnesa loved numbers;
history numbers
geography numbers,
science numbers,
but mostly, math numbers;
decimals
        angles
                divisors
                        ratios

It was a tough fifth grade year
for wordy little me.

# Unwanted Gifts

*Poem written after Ruth Grotenrath's painting, "Puncinello"*

He stopped by the Farmer's Market this morning
bought me irises from the neighbor's booth.
Loosed from their brown paper wrapping,
they await the blue vase, water-filled,
on my crazy orange counter,
their deep purple petals, floral velvet.

But now Puncinello,
my gray cat, approaches,
and I can tell by his intense stare
that these flowers will not long live here
I already know he feels
the same about the gentleman.

Francha Barnard

# Veil

*for Deanna*

Her father died in February.
His daughter now rocks in the slow-swinging
hammock of mourning.

She has lived long enough to know him,
to know his faults and virtues.
And so their story is not a fairytale
but neither is it a Greek tragedy.

Though one day she'll leave the hammock,
fold it and box it for other griefs,
she'll still always wear the veiled scar
of knife-nicked love for her father.

# Paper Pulp

Filtered sunlight
Pours fresh gold cream
On risotto slurry,
Warms water
Cooled by last night's
Starry sleep.

Eager hands
Slide silently in
To stir again
The sauce.
Paper art today,
A generous soup indeed.

Francha Barnard

# Gravity

The way it splashes and tumbles
water's liquid beneficence
from mountain heights to valley floors.

The way it fills the bowls of lakes.

The way it buoys my kayak today
on this last paddle of the season.

The way it aids these brilliant leaves
to drift down from the arms of trees.

The way it, oh!
temporarily tethers two bald eagles
to the rocky point of this ancient pier
as I round it, close enough
to see the yellow of their eyes.

The way it rivers a tear
down my cheek
on this October morning.

# Celebration Dinner

*Dress up, he said. We're going out
to celebrate your birthday.*
We drove uptown, valet-parked,
waltzed up to the maître-de
in a tiny mid-block bistro
where a signal from my escort
secured us a corner table.

He promptly ordered for us;
didn't let me see the menu.
I will, in retrospect, observe,
the service was impeccable.

The appetizer floated in,
a small bed of arugula for
three perfect tiny shrimp, grilled lightly,
drizzled with creole glacé

followed by the main course,
a single glistening sea scallop
atop a Stilton-filled portobello cap
on a shredded carrot hillock,
laced with warm ginger-pepper cream.

The palate-cleansing salad
was placed before us next—
a tiny plate of precious greens
with a light balsamic drizzle
and five (I counted them),
candied walnut pieces.

Yes, there was dessert—
a golf ball of just-made ice cream

Francha Barnard

plum/jasmine, distinctly floral,
napped with salted almond crumbles;
a tiny spoon for eating.

Every course was palate bliss
and, still, I had to question,
(only to myself, of course),
"Is that all there is?"
This Wisconsin girl went home hungry.

## My Dear Women of the Word,

This morning in early sun
I write you to say aloud
how your loyalty and interest
have buoyed me on our poets' journey.

You've taught me to wait
and listen
and watch,
then write.

Today the lake's tiny wavelets
are dancing in sparkles,
the house wrens and red-eyed vireos
sing their eternal songs,
the apple tree's leaves
barely offer the "Queen's wave".

How could there not be a missive
for you in this soft air?

I wish for you this summer's benevolence
in wind's absence,
in water and wings and warmth.

Francha Barnard

# Childhood Saturdays

So many Saturdays in deep winter were filled
in the mornings when the junior high one block away,
held open gym, then woodworking shop.
We grew to be good climbers on ropes and poles
and tool-users, too, sometimes with bandaged digits.
Afternoons often included a bus ride
downtown to the Central High pool.

But I remember most
the treat of Saturday night suppers
after leftover Thursday and fish on Friday.
The weekend always meant
hamburgers, chips and chocolate milk
all seen through red, burning eyes,
remnants of the afternoon's swim;
the lingering after-smell of chlorine
mixing with the sweet scent of grilled meat.

# Appetizer

It didn't start 'til adulthood,
this love of olives:
the shiny greens and blacks
of little rounds and ovals,
the bite of slightly resistant skin,
the soft interior surrounding stone
(or maybe not, if pitted earlier),
the residual oily mouthfeel,
the satisfaction, the temptation.

Kalamatas and nicoise,
liguria and picholine —
they all live in my cupboard,
eager soldiers to be marched out single file
on the long and skinny pottery tray
of gold and blue and green,
to seduce my guests as I have been seduced.

Francha Barnard

# To the Barre

*for Mrs. Finst, my ballet teacher*

We were a long way
from tutus and diaphanous dresses
on those cold winter Saturday mornings
when we'd climb the steep stairs
to the second floor of the old Eagles Hall
and enter the tiny changing room
where we'd trade boots for ballet slippers
then HUSH
as we'd tiptoe through the narrow archway
into a long-mirrored room that was our studio.

Backs straight, we'd line up – eight to the barre
and begin the work – week after week
first position, second position, third position,
fourth position, fifth position,
*eleve', plie', battement tendu,*
that would transform tomboys into graceful swans,

or so our mothers hoped.

# Siren Call

*siren call: from Greek mythology – the enticing appeal of something alluring but potentially dangerous*

It can't be said she always lived
a life defined by sorrow;
certainly not when the war was on
and she, a high school senior.
The USO was a siren's call
for townies and boys far from home.

But, oh, when it once began,
the heavy rope bound tight
always her heart in sorrow
and never loosed its knot.

She birthed the child, a girl,
when she was just past being one herself;
could not endure the shame
and pain of raising it alone.
Town was small and talk flew fast,
She gave it up to strangers.

Now, a fading eighty-five,
she lies on her hospice bed at home,
readies herself to journey on
to whatever the next life holds for her,
feels still sorrow's binding rope,
whispers good-by to her lost child.

Francha Barnard

How can I know this story is true?
I can't; it's one I just make up
to wrap around me on dark nights.
I am the child she gave away.

# Sinking

*Poem written after Dave Tilton's painting,
"Lake Ice III"*

As the sun rose behind reluctant clouds
we could see where she rested, a shadow only,
just below the surface in shallow water.

We knew we were to blame.
Eighteen, and made reckless
by summer beer,
we'd run the boat last night
out beyond the harbor,
then through chop until
she drank so much water
we couldn't bail fast enough
to keep ourselves afloat.
She sank on the shelf of a sandbar.

*So it is with all our stories –
waiting just below the surface
to be raised and written.*

Francha Barnard

# Adopted

This is a poem about not being
a poem about a genealogy that's not mine

about a Dutch grandmother with three daughters
whose hands crocheted string potholders I still use today

a widow most of her years
my grandfather felled in the flu epidemic

about a grandmother who died too soon
birthing her second child;

a grandfather searching for and finding
another mother for his two sons,

about my own mother raised by her mother
skilled in all domestic arts

about my father who learned to love reading
and passed that love to his brood of five

about a family I'm lucky to claim
but nonetheless know its chain is not mine

Down My Fairy Stairs

# First Library

There was that long low bench
at the back of the branch library
one block from home.
There were those long low bookshelves
under large windows.

In our children's corner,
the wood shone warm
as through the many panes above us,
light, always in my memory, filtered gold
and below it, our picture books,
lined up like waiting wafers,
for us to devour them.

And, as an additional visual treat,
the bottom shelf held stereoscopes
with boxes and boxes
of double-vision photo cards.

But the books, oh, the books,
that opening world of discovery;
dear Ferdinand, spunky Christopher Robin,
the feisty monkeys of *Caps for Sale*,
Peter Rabbit who was so like us,
the Swedish siblings, Flicka, Ricka and Dicka
and their male counterparts, Snipp, Snapp and Snurr.

Then, when I was lucky and it was in,
the book I checked out again and again,
*Hat for a Hero*—about a brave, very short child.
Oh, why did I especially like that one?

Francha Barnard

Thanks to our corner in that library,
we neighborhood kids were readers
and adventurers far beyond
the boundaries of our nearby houses.

# Expiration Date: A Brief Encounter

There is a certain look
about the dying.
In nursing homes this is well-known
for there is no other exit.

Now it was Clara, my mother's
neighbor across the hall,
sweet, cheerful, vibrant Clara,
who had begun her journey out.

I'd brought Sabrina, tiny old white kitty,
to visit with my ailing mom;
saw Clara lying, eyes shut, breath shallow
and took Sabrina there instead.

I placed my ghost-cat on Clara's bed,
beside her now so still body.
Slowly, slightly, an old hand lifted
and rested on Sabrina's back.

Though Clara died that evening,
I like to think Sabrina
helped to spirit dear Clara
to her destination.

Francha Barnard

# Old Blue Patchwork

In the late-night hours
she cocoons under the antique quilt.
Some of its squares
have long surrendered their fill.
All of its squares are faded blues,
faded by use in shirts,
and dresses before they ever
became this quilt,
its work not yet finished,
that covers the bed
that looks on the lake.

Her body warms
beneath its simple patchwork
of checks, plains and prints
as it has for all
these Door County years
since she brought it here,
already old.

## Section B

*"Tonight I saw myself in the dark window as the image of my father"* Louise Gluck

Yesterday I chose my cemetery plot.
Long lines of relatives skimmed in my head,
great aunts who raised my father for six years
while my grandfather found a new wife,
a godmother, cherished for fun and travel,
my mother's mother, always a lady,
my own mother who lived her mother's example,
that grandfather who built a home
here on the lake -- a house of play and laughter
for his grandchildren.

Then last night late, there was me in the mirror,
child not of my parents born,
choosing to be buried away from family,
but where I feel most grounded, most planted.

Always I thought not birth,
but environment had formed me
and made me most like my mother,
social, involved, organizer, volunteer.
Now though, shuttered by Covid
I see I'm more my father's child,
content to be alone,
finding my pleasure in books,
in both imagination and facts, in reflection.

The urn that will be lowered
into the earth of lot 54,
this amalgam that is me turned to ash
will have a quiet space

Francha Barnard

near a crabapple tree —
two requests my father made
for his own final rest beside Lake Superior.

# Old Cat

*"What's grown so loved is gone to ground."*
*from Bruce Dethlefsen's Poem "Gone to Ground"*

Everything about her was soft;
her name, Arianna,
her long *tortie* fur
her tentative pink tongue,
her reticence and,
on her final morning,
the way she softly lay her head down
and let life go.

Francha Barnard

# The Seatmate

There is a certain luxury
in NOT striking up a conversation
on a train.
It leaves one free to speculate –

Who is this Scotsman of a certain age
who sits now, facing me
on this late afternoon
train into Glasgow,

umbrella hooked on his elbow;
folder in his lap
blond hair gone that muddy gray,
combed long over his ears –

slim frame,
sweatered and suited and tied
in the moss green/gray
I imagine men of Scotland favor.

And the face, such an interesting face – lean, lined,
eyebrowed with a thick fringe
of unruly white;
water-blue eyes above
a strong nose and equally strong lips.

Could he be a musician
going into the city to play?
Long fingers with well-trimmed nails
hint at that.

Too mild, I think, for professor,
but then,

Down My Fairy Stairs

there are many types
drawn to teach.

In this city
of architecture,
could he be an architect?
He does appear a detail man.

Oh, he's writing now in a notebook,
tiny like this one –
making, I see, minuscule notations
on Moleskin pages.

I know,
he's a poet, and a lefty, too,
writing a poem about me
as I write one of him.

Francha Barnard

# This Year's Letter

Santa,
You dear old busy man,
my roof doesn't need a stop this year.
I'll just be asking once again
for health in the days to come.

You brought it last year,
though I didn't know then
health would be the gift delayed
'til this annual holiday time.

You could just fling it
on your night flight past
and I'll thank you daily
in the year ahead.

Fondly,
Francha

Will's Summer People
Door County

Francha Barnard

# Will's Summer People

*Bjorklunden, Baileys Harbor*

One ambled by on the road last night
and I began to wonder,
how many actors and actresses,
scripts in hand,
had walked this way before,
reading lines,
rehearsing gestures,
framing faces of levity or gravity.

How many—days later—came by again,
scriptless now, lost inside their own heads?
For them, our woods—the forests of Arden or Birnam Wood;
this lake—the ocean that tossed Prospero and Miranda ashore;
this sky—the deep night wonder after the wedding at Padua
or the trickery in the fairy forest of Titania and Oberon.

For them, no doubt,
this road will always hold
a larger world,
an older world,
a world cast in Will's creation.

# A Beep and a Wave

*Baileys Harbor, 2017*

Tutus of ice pirouette near shore
this February morning
of sun and single digits.
Snowbirds have long flown south
and those of us who stay
on this frigid peninsula
cross paths often,
play, challenge our minds,
make art and poems;
heeding, but rarely conceding
to winter's vagaries.

Walking in town often brings
a beep and a wave;
unspoken tribute from neighbors
of the friendship and fortitude we share
in this tiny town on the lake.

Francha Barnard

# Overlooked

*Poem written after Fred Perryman's painting
"Distant County Haze"*

Alone on a stairway wall
inconspicuous
almost incongruous,
corralled by the gallery's
many large pieces commanding attention,
this small oil,
two blue-green trees, deciduous,
maybe summer maples,
stand as if parent and child,
the little one leaning in,
stand alone on flat ground, unmanicured,
a mildly clouded scrim, their horizon.

This would be a place
too often passed without notice.
This would be an invitation
to remember the overlooked,
to honor quiet, unobtrusive things.
They call in whispers.

# Weavers

*for the Hickey Brothers fishermen*

They stand side by side
in the low-ceilinged shack;
two strong young men
practicing an old man's art.

Net pulled to line,
hold tight,
over, around and through.

Gossamer nets hang low between them.
Two taut nylon lines stretch
waist-high through the room
attached to opposite walls.

Ten phrases of six,
then three on the float,
over, around and through.

Bobbins in hand, they snail-pace backwards,
catch net to line and tie it tight,
eyes never lifting; rhythm unbroken,
hours a day, days for weeks.

Ten phrases of six,
then three on the lead,
over, around and through.

Summertime catchers of fish;
wintertime menders of nets,
from their deft hands grow new webs:
Arachne's opus before Athena's ire.

Francha Barnard

# May Ritual

*or, The Mating Imperative of Certain Amphibians*

They're partying hard
near the Kangaroo Causeway
peeping their throats sore
to celebrate spring.

*Just maybe*

earlier binge drinking
at the Coyote Roadhouse
loosened their pipes
and all inhibitions.

*Now*

everybody's talking
and nobody's listening –
except for lake humans
who won't sleep well tonight.

## At Hidden Brook

Maybe it was raining hard,
drops plopping on the windows,
maybe it was windy,
leaf dervishes whirling on the lawn,
maybe breakers were rolling in
blanketed by a gray scrim,
maybe flakes drifted down,
each different and chilling.

It didn't matter whether the weather
was fraught or fey,
my Grandpa's front hall entry,
ceiling not painted but back-lit
in glowing azure and pearl
from a slice of blue sky with
cumulus mounding
raised our eyes, our spirits.

Francha Barnard

# Good Luck

When I was young
and lived in a city,
on early morning runs
in spring and summer
I'd mark the day's luck
with the rabbits I saw.

A one-bunny morning
meant a good day ahead;
two-bunny mornings
were better;
and three-bunny mornings,
well…

Now I'm old
and live in the country.
Good luck collateral here
is Papa fox on my terrace
most evenings
and now and then,
an eagle morning.

# Tamaracks

It's the afternoon of the harvest ball;
the tall girls are donning their golden gowns,
twirling this way and that
coyly glancing over their shoulders
and checking their reflections
in the Three Springs mirror.
They've heard Jack's coming home
to the palace just for the dance.
He's been far away for so many months,
but whispers are claiming he's lately
been charming the girls up north.

Everyone knows long after he's offered his
crystal bangles to the other Cinderellas;
after they've preened and posed,
commanded attention in their reds and rusts,
dipped and dashed off coy kisses,
whirled around the dance floor
and out the palace door to their 12 o'clock beds,
the tamaracks will still be standing golden tall
at the edge of the dance floor
eager to be the true princesses
of the wee hours of the ball.

Francha Barnard

# Walking Home from Shakespeare

*Bjorklunden, Door County*

A humid August evening, late,
Kate, that shrew —
that liberated woman —
depending on how
you judge her,
has filled the Garden
with haughty angst
as Petruchio
worked to woo her.

The story's ended;
we've started for home
muffled chuckles
at lines remembered,
walking back-paths
just as in Padua
caped in darkness,
moon not yet risen—
only a torch's feeble beam
and sky's starry umbrella
to reveal our way.
It could be Italy
after the wedding.

Half the fun of going
is in the coming home.

# Fog-marked Morning

*Poem written after Ginnie Cappaert's painting "Summer Solstice"*

Summer comes late to this peninsula
particularly along the lake's edges;
dolomite limestone holds water's cold,
clammy dense fog lingers long.

This morning, even close to shore,
fishing boats are shrouded, funereal.
All that betrays their passing is
the low thrum-hum of their motors.

They skirt the aqua-green shallows,
keep to the darker blues of deep water,
steer clear of skeletons of earlier ships
less marked by fortune than they.

From their wet decks, though,
the early fishers find land's line,
slate-ochre rocks shelved high,
skeletal birch and cedar trunks.

Lifting eyes upward
they see the milky mustard
of an early working sun
leaning in on the slow-fading grey.

Francha Barnard

# Dancing Cows

As you drive north on 57
slow down just before County I
and glance east....to the farm of dancing cows.

If you're lucky you'll see them scoot
from the standard red barn near the house
and romp down a slight incline
to their lower pasture stage.

You'll notice the skip in their step,
the smiles on their bovine faces
as they gather below near the road,
black and white crowding closer together.

You'll see front feet leave the ground
then back feet follow in kind.
You may even see some cows
 with all four feet in the air at once.

Holstein popcorn
dancing delight to invisible music.
How lovely, how magic, how free.

# A Sensual Sunset

*Poem written after Judi Ekholm's painting "Edges: Peninsula State Park"*

We're so often on edges in a landscape.
Here, the earth/sky, water/land, day/night.
Listen, do you hear amid raucous reds and oranges,
the closing of the day
the creeping hush of night
on this beach in Peninsula Park?

Of course darkness never brings silence
in woods, on water.
Lapping wavelets and settling birds
underline the evening.
In Ekholm's painting, as day exits,
she vamps her brightest, loudest
across the bay's water
setting it aflame if only for minutes,
casting deep shadows behind tall grasses
before fading on the shore to near black,
casting a cape of peace over us who watch.

Francha Barnard

# Honor System Shopping

In a handcart at the edge of a yard
three houses west on County EE
a bounty appears in late July
and reappears daily 'til the end of fall.
Though the farmer is never seen,
you can follow the harvest by crops in his cart.

First, mixed lettuce—at least six kinds in purple and green,
each offering a different shape, tang and bite.
Then broccoli, tight new baby heads,
carrots that taste like carrots, fat and sunrise orange,
beets, their long greens peeking from a bucket,
cabbages, red and white and heavy,
parsnips on lucky days, ready for roasting.
cauliflower heads of creamy white and gold.
Last, squashes; butternut, patty pan, acorn
and pumpkins for carving or others for baking.

Tiny prices appear on each piece—
all paid on the honor system in a wide-mouthed jar
for your coins and bills or for making change,
another with bags to ferry home your load.

No corn though—
his brothers on the farm around the corner
specialize in that,
fill a wheelbarrow of cobs and replenish it often.
Same honor system used for payment.

# The Neighbor's Cows

Sturdy,
that's what I like about them,
they're sturdy;
feet firmly planted,
black and white marks
warranting a second glance,
they hardly move
or not at all.

And their legs –
I like to watch the knees
bending as they begin to plod,
walking-sticks below that bulk,
especially crossing
the country road to home in the evening;
stopping and looking,
making me stop to look.

Francha Barnard

# Zukes and Cukes

*Poem written after Tom Nachreiner's painting
"Farmers' Veggies"*

Under the weight of garden largess
our autumn Farmers' Market tables
groan with the pleasure of presentation,
purples of eggplant, tomato reds,
greens of cukes and zukes,
pearly whites of fat round onions,
their stems still telling the story
of months spent underground.

Here they are,
heaped on the home table
from the bag that brought them,
more full than intended.

Their scent of soil
and bracing autumn air
fills the kitchen
and heads of those shoppers
who just brought them here,
their future uses,
beyond their beauty,
already dancing in imaginations.

# Certainty

*Written after the tall ship, Unicorn,
moored in Baileys Harbor 2013*

Science notwithstanding,

we children who grew up
on Lake Michigan's long shore
knew, because we'd seen them,
that sharks lived in the water.

We saw their fins, slow gliding,
reflected in bright sunlight
and though we were told otherwise,
knew those weren't just shiny wavelets.

History notwithstanding,

our old eyes last week saw the schooner,
black-hulled and two-masted
as she glided in at twilight,
no wind abroad to sail her,

dropped anchor at our bay's lip,
lit her lamps below-deck
and we knew the skull and crossbones
were hidden in her furled sails

So we tell our stories.
We believe if none else do.
Who really knows the borderline –
what is false and what is true?

Francha Barnard

# Tuesday, 4:32 a.m.

*after Basho*

The wind is asleep.
The crickets are asleep.
Even the waves are asleep.

Now a low, throttle-down
rumbles across the bay
of this ancient Silurian Sea.

The Hickey Brothers fishing boats
are heading out to gain early purchase
on the day's silent swimmers.

## Pencil in Hand

July.
Summer has just simmered
to the top of the pot
at The Ridges.
It is good to sit awhile
at Solitude Swale,
its glassy water silent.

But that's the only silence here.
Invisible bullfrogs bassoon their songs
red darners skim just above the surface
iridescent bluets dart to and fro
both add their underlying zooms.

Each scene on the swale,
a confetti of ideas,
flits, glides, comes to light
but not to land
as the poet attempts to capture
and hold this ephemeral afternoon.

Francha Barnard

# Just Before the Hunt

The trails of the Ridges today
are replete with hoofprints,
tiny, mirrored crescents and
larger, deeper twin impressions.

Silence, but for birdcall,
veils the lacy cedars.

How many, I wonder, of the mark-makers
will no longer be with us tomorrow
when the veil is rent
by rifle fire.

# Talisman

Papa Fox never really leaves
though he's been gone for five or six years,
taken by mange that swept through
the wild canines of Door County,
taking raccoons, coyote and yes, foxes.

He is, I've long accepted
the talisman of my life here,
in my mind nearly daily, as he was
in life on the terrace each night.

How do we reconcile the wild in our lives?
Do our hearts ever stop breaking
for the beauty, the courage,
the connection?

Francha Barnard

# Survivor

Skinny baby red oak
planted here in early June
wears this morning one last leaf
before her winter sleep begins.

Chosen for her strength to thrive
through future weather changes;
higher heat, more rain and snow
on this northern peninsula,

she'll need roots to tunnel deep,
hug the rocky limestone soil,
drink when drink falls from the sky,
eat of this headland's earth and air.

Today, though,
as the wind is laughing,
her summer frock drops to the floor.
Her bones dance in the nude.

Francha Barnard

# I Do Begrudge Losing Dappled Days

The lake has eaten my fairy stairs—
at their entrance, a low cedar archway.
Down, first, eight narrow steps,
the cliff wall, karst-cracked,
so close I could touch it;
a turn at the landing to a view of our bay.
Down ten more then
to a paltry stone beach
and my kayak kept there
to turn, float and go.

Gone now, August and September swimming
   in sun-warmed waves, rough stones for our sand.
Gone coffee, mornings on the bottom step;
   wine, on numbered smudgy summer evenings.
Gone, too, private or step-shared,
   sunrises, moonrises some scarlet on water.
Gone that space away from the world
   where silence ruled on waveless days.
Gone that extravagant decade of poetry
   not written or spoken but lived.

## About the Author

Francha Barnard

July 6, 1946 – July 22, 2022

Francha Barnard was a full-time resident of Baileys Harbor, WI for 17 years following her retirement in 2005 as an elementary school librarian. She said of herself, "I play at art, and work at poetry". Francha submitted her poetry on a regular basis, and her poems appeared in local publications with "Weavers" winning the 1$^{st}$ place award in the *Peninsula Pulse's Hal Grutzmacher's Writers' Expose poetry contest* in 2010. Many other poems were selected for the *Wisconsin Poets' Calendar*, including her ode to Frogtown Road, "A Beep and a Wave." Her artistic endeavors ranged from fiber arts, such as weaving, to collage and jewelry making. Door County was her true love.

Francha was a daughter, sister, good neighbor, best friend, literary citizen and champion for those who could not speak for themselves. Foremost she was a fighter, to the very end.

# About the Illustrator

Elizabeth Ann Barnard is a self-taught artist whose passion lies in the 3D representation of objects on a 2D surface, with drawing and watercolor being her primary interests. Family, hiking, cooking, yoga, Pilates, reading and writing, beach and mountain trips, and tending to her spiritual nature occupy most of her time. A Sheboygan, WI native she has lived nearly half her life in North Carolina with her life-long partner, Steve. She misses Francha every day.

www.ingramcontent.com/pod-product-compliance
Lightning Source LLC
Chambersburg PA
CBHW052030030426
42337CB00027B/4941